Adulting 101: The Things They Don't Teach You
Copyright © 2018 by Erin Clark. All Rights Reserved.

Published by CLC Publishing, LLC, Oklahoma City, OK
Published in the United States of America

Cover Design by

ISBN: 978-1717315700

Non-Fiction – Self-Help – Motivation

Erin A. Clark

Adulting 101: The Things They Don't Teach You

By Erin A. Clark

Erin A. Clark

Contents

Erin A. Clark

Prologue

I remember graduating High school and assuming my life would go according to plan. Here was my plan: I'd go to college, graduate, get my dream job right away, fall in love, get married, buy a house, and have 2.5 kids and a dog. Why did I assume this? Maybe because it has been engrained in my head since I was a kid watching Disney movies and sitcoms. That's just was how life was supposed to work out. Maybe because I saw my parents' and grandparents' lives and assumed mine would follow that exact path. However, that's not exactly how it worked out. But, I wouldn't know that until actually living my life and finding out that life doesn't always go according to plan; and everyone's life follows a different trajectory.

The path to living a happy and fulfilling life is not straight and easy. It's filled with bumps and potholes, and if your driving skills are anything like mine, you're probably going to get pulled over or crash at least a few times. I'm still driving on my metaphorical road and I've crashed a few times, but I feel like I've learned a lot and I want to help you learn. The desire to help you learn from my mistakes and avoid my potholes comes from a combination of different things.

The first was turning 25. Right before my 25th birthday, I had a series of mini-panic attacks because I realized that 25 is an adult age. I was, gulp, officially an adult. As someone who rarely worries and had never actually had a panic attack, you can imagine my relief when I realized that panic attacks don't just come with age. But I wasn't panicking because I felt old, or because I found a grey hair (although that didn't exactly make me feel young and beautiful) but because I realized that there are so many "adult" things that I don't know how to do – either they were never taught to me, or I simply never learned. I must have been absent from school the day they taught how to organize or budget your money. There were so many things that I didn't know how to do; how to do my taxes, save money, grocery shop, build healthy relationships, cleaning/organizing, time management, how important establishing and building good credit is...the list goes on and on. I got through my panic attacks because I have a great group of friends who assured me that they had no idea what they were doing either. In fact, the more people I talked to, particularly those in my generation, the more I realized that almost NO ONE knows what they're doing. No one knows how to "adult." You see, there's no guidebook that comes with a high school diploma or arrives in your dorm during freshman orientation that provides life lessons for you. And if you're waiting for an adult pamphlet to arrive, and suddenly you turn 25 and realize you're totally unprepared, you might also feel a little overwhelmed. And this book may be just what you need!

I learned many lessons the hard way; no, in case you were wondering, you can't avoid doing laundry for months on end by just buying new clothes. I've tried, you will run out of money. And many other things have been taught to me by inspirational mentors and leaders. In college, I was fortunate enough to find a sales job that taught me so many skills, other than selling. I remember going to one of my first work conferences – with blazers and all – and learning about how to save money and how to set up a Roth IRA. I remember thinking, and complaining afterwards, *"Why didn't anyone teach me this before?!"* I want you to have as few of those moments as possible. Fair warning, though, I'm not an expert. I don't know everything, and I'm still learning, but I can at least tell you some of the things I've learned. There's a very good chance that I'll look back on this book 10 years from now and think "Silly, Erin. You didn't know what you were talking about," but by then I'll have 10 more years of experiences, lessons and funny or slightly embarrassing stories to share. But, those will be for another book!

We are the generation of no child left behind where standardized testing was always the norm and any student can tell you the Pythagorean Theorem but can't tell you how to budget or write a check. We are the generation of Myspace, Facebook and Twitter and anyone can tell you which emoji to use, but they can't choose the right business professional outfit for a job interview. I'm here to help you defy stereotypes and be the exception to the "lazy" generation.

So, this book is for YOU, the twenty-two-year-old eating peanut butter out of the jar for dinner because no one taught you how to cook. This book is for YOU, the 18-yearold high school grad who is struggling to save money for college. This book is for YOU, the 25-year-old currently having an existential crisis because you don't feel like you're where you should be in life. This book is for YOU, from me: someone who has been in all those situations and has survived. This is your survival guide.

Expectation vs. Reality

"If you align your expectations with reality, you will never be disappointed." Terrell Owens

A lot of the panic I was experiencing stemmed from comparing what I expected to happen and what was really happening in my life. Jobs and degrees aside, what about friends? What about my social life? I realized that I'm 25 and hardly have a life. Isn't this supposed to be the time where I'm young, wild and free? This is the time of my life, right? I think a lot of being an adult is considering going out to a bar or concert, but then deciding to stay inside where you can stay in your yoga pants and drink wine with your cat. I know I'm not alone in that thought. Now, I'm not some kind of hermit, although sometimes I consider running away, building a cabin somewhere in the backwoods of New Hampshire and cutting myself off from civilization entirely. I don't consider myself to be socially awkward, I just like time to myself once in a while. I've always been known as an extrovert. Teachers throughout high school and college, bosses and even my clients express to me that I'm wellspoken, friendly, I've even been called charismatic. But I'm realizing the older I get, the harder it is to make and keep friends. People who signed my high school year book with "Keep in touch" or even the stereotypical "BFFs" haven't talked to me, other than the occasional Facebook post of "Happy Birthday, Hope you're well," in years. And I can't be mad at them, I haven't exactly reached out to them either.

There was a time in college where I talked to some of my old high school friends. We even met up for margaritas a few times. But life, as they say, got in the way. Our schedules are different, we work so much, we have new groups of friends etc. and before I know what has even happened, 3 years have gone by and suddenly they're married and having children or are moving across the country.

I'm not trying to scare you. If you're in high school and thinking "my high school friends really are my best friends, Erin, you don't know what you're talking about," that's fine. I'm not saying *all* of your friends are going to abandon you the second you step on a college campus. My roommate has not only kept in touch with her high school friends but has been in their weddings and still considers them to be her best friends. And if your high school friends are true friends, it's worth keeping them in your favorite section in your phone. But sometimes, losing touch with old friends is ok – especially if they weren't really your friends in the first place. Your twenties are the perfect time to branch out and make new friends. Or, you might realize that you, too, want to be a hermit and join me in my cabin filled with cats (all animals are welcome!) and that's ok, too. But you should still find your squad, even if it's one other person who has your back at all times.

Surround yourself with good people. You are the average of the five people you spend the most time with. Take a second to evaluate your circle. Do those people have traits that you aspire to have? Again, there are always exceptions. But if you're in a not-so-good place and are not happy with where you are in life, it could be because your friends are negging you out. I'm not saying abandon your circle of friends and never talk to them. But maybe just spend less time with your friend who is constantly negative or complaining all the time and more time with the friend who lifts you up, motivates you and makes you laugh. Surround yourself with greatness and you will be great. "Surround yourself with dreamers and the doers, the believers and thinkers, but most of all, surround yourself with those who see greatness within you, even when you don't see it yourself." ~Edmond Lee

Now you might be realizing, "wait a minute, the negative person in my group is someone I'm related to!" Now what? Again, you're not abandoning them. Family is family, after all. But if your cousin is constantly complaining, or even worse bringing you down, try talking to them. If you find yourself repeatedly asking "hey, maybe you could be a little more positive," maybe you just need to spend less time with them.

I'm so happy that I was born into the family I was because I'm surrounded by love and support, (and I'm not saying that because they're all going to read this, really). My mom was one of four and my dad was one of five, and each of their brothers and sisters had 2-3 children, so to say that I have a lot of cousins is an understatement. Even better is that all of my cousins are near my age, so I grew up with immediate friends. But even my family has grown and separated slightly over time. We're all working, or in college, or busy with finals, or moving in with a new person. Again, life gets in the way. We're still in touch through Facebook and Snap Chat and other social media but suffice it to say we're not as close as we once were. About a year ago, I got stuck in comparing my life to others. And I was really hard on myself because the people I was comparing my life to were some of the people I'm closest to. A lot of my cousins were finishing grad school or getting their PHDs. I felt like the black sheep of the family for having no desire to go back to school and being ok living my life with only a bachelor's degree. Even though that's actually a really good accomplishment and I graduated debt free and with honors, I still didn't feel accomplished because I was comparing what I'd done to what others were doing. I found myself thinking "Should I go to grad school? But I don't know what I'd go for. Is it worth the money?" I had to talk it out. I learned to focus on what I *had* done instead of what I hadn't (even if that is something I don't actually want to do). Since then, I've learned that my life is my own. If I decide to go to grad school, that's great. But I don't ever want to feel like I have to do something just because other people are doing that.

Sometimes doing your own thing and focusing on you can be hard. Sometimes the toughest decision you will face will be choosing to be selfish. But sometimes, that is necessary. The older I get, the more I realize that I can't make decisions for anyone else. This is especially hard if you're like me and seek to please as many people as possible. You can't please everyone all the time. You have to figure out what you want, and you have to make conscious decisions to go after it. If you really want something, you'll find a way; If you don't you'll find an excuse. Here's an example you might come across: your goal is to get all A's for a semester, but every Thursday, Friday and Saturday your friends go out and invite you along. You have a choice, go out with them to please their social needs or decide to be selfish and stay in and study. It's ok to make the decision to go out once in a while, but you're definitely going to regret going out every night when the end of the semester rolls around and you have a lot of work to catch up on. Again, if all of your friends are partiers, maybe seek out new friends in a study group.

Lessons Learned

It's ok to branch out, make new friends, or even realize that it's ok to spend the night in occasionally. Surround yourself with positive people and don't get so caught up in comparing your story to someone else's that you forget to live your own story.

Adulting Tactic #1

Are you surrounding yourself with good people? Ask yourself: Is my circle lifting me up, or pulling me down? What can I do to better my circle? There are many ways to answer this question and everyone is different. Maybe the answer to this, for you, is that you need to branch out, network and intentionally make connections with people who lift you up.

Maybe you just need to talk to your friend who unintentionally says something that leaves you doubtful.

Baby Boomers vs. Millennials

"Can you remember who you were before the world told you who you should be?" Danielle LaPorte

Dealing with Anxiety

Another way to get stuck in the comparison cycle is comparing our generation to our parents'. The Millennials vs. the Baby Boomers. We hear these terms thrown around a lot. There are differences between every generation, of course. But it seems that lately there has been a huge emphasis on this "millennial" generation, those reaching young adulthood in the early 2000s, and what we have done wrong, or rather what's working against us. Just google the term. Article after article, you'll see "5 ways millennials are like no generation before them" or "The unluckiest generation." You can read the articles, but I'll save you some time: the main difference between our generation and the generations before us is security.

When my parents graduated high school, it was almost guaranteed that they'd go to college and afterwards, get a job in the field in which they studied. That job was secure.

In fact, most people in the generation before us have worked in the same field, or even the same job for 20 plus years. Someone who jumped from job to job was a rarity. Because their job was secure, they didn't worry where they'd be in 20 years. They were comfortable investing in homes and putting savings away.

Our generation doesn't have the same cushion and cozy blanket known as security. The terms "job security" and "savings" are only used in panic or are a total foreign concept. The terms "debt" and "student loans" are much more common. This results in endless penny scraping, nervousness, and lack of savings. The fact is, there are no guarantees now. Nothing is secure. The fact that you went to college is no longer your ticket to success. It is very rare, among people in my generation, that you find someone who actually has a job in a field they went to school for.

Yes, the lack of security is scary, but it's not always a bad thing. I have my BA in English and have a great job in sales. No, I'm not getting paid for what I studied (unless of course you, reader, buy thousands of copies of this book to give to every single one of your friends). I started this job while I was in college, intending to work there just for a summer. But I did well and discovered I'm good at it. So that's the job that pays the bills, and I'm able to use the skills I acquired in college. Nothing is guaranteed, but that's not always a bad thing. The unexpected is going to happen, that's inevitable – it's how you handle the unexpected that matters.

No one expects to be serving pumpkin spice lattes after working hard to complete their degree for four years. No one expects to be living with their parents nearly two years

AFTER they've graduated. But there's two ways to look at those situations. You can either be mopey and sad because a 23-year-old isn't "supposed" to be living with their parents.

Or you can look at it as the best temporary situation while you save money. And you shouldn't feel bad that you're fortunate enough to have parents that love you and allow you to stay with them. Understandably, your fierce independence is going to come through and there are going to be times when you want nothing more than your own place and to make your own rules but have patience. Your savings account will thank you.

As the generation deemed "unlucky," it's difficult to stay positive. If you're constantly comparing your life to your parents', or even your friends, you're going to feel overwhelmed. But you have to remember: we are coming to adulthood in a totally different time than the generation before us. When my parents were 25, they were already married, owned a home and had 2 kids (and another one to come within 2 years). With those facts in my mind as I scrolled Facebook one day and realized that nearly all of my Facebook friends my age are either engaged, married, buying a home, or having kids, I freaked. I mean really, a full freak out complete with tears (probably enhanced by the wine I was drinking for dinner) and anxiety. This was right before my 25th birthday. And as someone who never really suffered from anxiety and had never had a panic attack in her life, I did NOT handle it well. I kind of went into shut down mode. I spent a few days watching Netflix and not doing anything. I complained and complained, I cried a little more, I drank more wine. None of that solved my problem though. The problem was that I was about to turn 25, but I didn't *feel* like an adult. I wasn't ready! How can I be an adult?! I still watch Disney movies for fun, I sometimes eat peanut butter for dinner, I hate doing laundry, I don't know how to change a tire, I'm certainly not ready to get married and I especially wouldn't be able to buy a home. Then I realized that technically speaking, I've been an adult for years! That resulted in even more panic. I was a mess. And all this from comparing my life and my current situation to what I thought I should have done or accomplished. It took a lot to come to terms with the fact that aging is inevitable. Whether I like it or not, my birthday was going to come. This was the very first year that I was not looking forward to my Birthday. This, to me, was a sure sign that I was now an adult.

I found the best way to cope with untangling the mess I found myself in was to talk it out. That's how I like to solve most of my problems. I talked to my roommate who assured me it would get better. I talked to my friends who all had had that realization at some point. I talked to my business coach and mentors who said that even as they age, they never actually feel that number, time just goes by faster. I talked to my boyfriend at the time who reminded me of all that I have accomplished. No, I haven't bought a house yet, but I have traveled a lot and have had a lot of amazing experiences. Not many people my age can say that they've had management experience. Not many people my age can say that they've won vacations based on sales contests. I had to focus on the good. I had to look at what I have done, not what I wanted to do or might not do for a while.

When I feel that terrifying anxiety creeping in, there are a few things I do, maybe these will help you too:

1. I talk it out. As I mentioned, that's something that really helps me. Whether I'm talking to my girlfriends drinking wine or talking to my boyfriend over dinner, I'll just ramble until I find a solution. Even if a solution isn't found, or can't be found, I'll feel better getting everything off my chest, so to speak.

2. I write it out. Ever since I was a little girl, I would journal. If something made me mad, I'd journal. If something made me happy, I'd journal. If something exciting happened, I'd journal. If I didn't do anything all day, I'd journal. Journaling has helped me in almost every situation I've ever been in from having a crush on a boy, to running an office and having to make difficult business decisions. If this is something you want to do but have never done, just start small. You don't have to write a novel every time you have a feeling, although the more you journal, the more you'll find yourself being taken away with what you're writing. Journaling can be as simple as writing down: what happened and what was my reaction? Sometimes that's enough. There's something very symbolic about putting pen to paper, writing down what you're feeling or thinking and then closing the book on the subject, literally.

3. I work it out. I do something physical. I was a dancer all though high school and I loved being able to put all my teenage angst aside and move. I didn't have to think about what happened at school, I could focus on the choreography and the music. It was euphoric. I don't dance nearly as much as I did in the past, (although I should, I really miss all the

benefits of dancing) but sometimes I'll just turn on a good song and dance around like a lunatic. I may look crazy, but I'll feel immensely better afterwards. Nowadays, I've made working out part of my routine. This helps with over-all health (the healthier you are physically, the better you feel mentally), but also if I'm stressed or anxious or even bored. I'll go for a long walk to clear my head.

4. I try to eat right and stay hydrated. Again, when you feel good, your mind is good. I do love excessive amounts of peanut butter, chocolate, wine and a number of other things that are not good for me, but I'm not one to torture myself and never eat those things. I'll eat them, but I try to limit the bad stuff. Another sign of being an adult: enjoying the taste of healthy foods. I also love salads and sometimes I'll crave a kale smoothie. Try to follow the 80:20 rule. 80% of the time, I'll eat salad or smoothies and work out every day and drink only water. The other 20%, for example, when I'm on vacation, I'll treat myself to a frozen margarita or chocolate cake for dinner.

So, I talked it out. I took a breath. And I realized that I would be ok. You may have experienced a similar anxiety attack. Maybe you suffer from panic and anxiety often – the meltdown I had is something you experience on a weekly basis. Or maybe, like me, you never really worried about anything and suddenly you are worried about things that haven't even happened yet. Either way, remember, it is going to be ok. Find your outlet, maybe it's talking or journaling, or focusing on your health, find what works for you. Focus on the good. Focus on the things you can control. You can't control that ups and downs of the housing market, but you can control what you add to your own personal savings account. You can't control the fact that it seems like all of your Facebook friends are living the life you want to. But you can control how you let that effect you. Don't compare your behind the scenes footage with someone else's edited movie reel.

Careers:

I've mentioned a few times that many people in my generation go to college and graduate only to work in a café serving coffee or a popular fast food place serving fries. The reality is most people are working 2 or even 3 jobs to make ends meet or just to pay off those annoying college loans. That's ok. Look to the bright side of the situation: it's not ideal, but it's also not permanent. You're not going to be serving coffee forever. And in today's world sometimes you have to take what you can get: a job at McDonalds is sometimes better than having no job at all.

Take this time to dream, to plan. Say to yourself "Ok, I'm going to work here making ____ an hour until ____ is paid off and while I'm working here, I'm going to be proactive and apply to my dream job." And then, most importantly, do what you say you're going to do, and follow through. It's easy to get caught up in the day-to-day, the routine. What's difficult is to stay focused on the long-term goal (to be debtfree, or to save for ____), but I promise, sometimes the most difficult things are most worth it.

My current job, as I've mentioned, is in sales. I didn't grow up from a young age saying, "I hope I hit my sales quota every month," of course not. Even though my job isn't what

I pictured I'd be doing with my life at 25, I really do enjoy it. I have pride in what I'm selling, it is a great product, I get to work with great people and I also have a super flexible schedule that allows me to plan my time effectively so that I can focus on the things I've always wanted to do: like write. You have to make the most of the situation you're currently in.

Maybe your schedule isn't flexible, but you're happy with your paycheck at the end of the week. Maybe your boss is the worst person in the world, but you have some great work friends who make you laugh. Look to the positive. And if there is absolutely nothing you like about your job, you make lists but can't find one good thing, then leave. Find something else. It's your life, make your own decisions. There is no law that says you have to stay at a dead-end job that exhausts you and pays you peanuts. I think many of my friends who are my age just stay with their awful job because they think there's nothing better out there. There is a lot out there, even if the media is telling you that the job market is terrible. Sometimes, all you need is a connection.

Sometimes opportunities arise not because of what you know, but who you know. Today, networking is essential. My friend Hannah exemplifies why networking is so important, she has been able to build her career step by step and is currently living her dream because of her dedication to her passion, her commitment to the grind and her networking skills.

Hannah's story:

I met Hannah through a friend. When I moved to Maine for a management opportunity with my company, I needed a receptionist; someone to answer calls, schedule interviews and kindly greet applicants. My friend, Sarah, another manager, gave me the contact information of her college roommate, Hannah, who happened to live in Maine and who happened to need a job for the summer. I interviewed Hannah at a small coffee shop near her college and knew pretty much instantly that I'd want to hire her – she put off a friendly, cool vibe, that I knew would help my business and I knew I'd enjoy working with. I was Hannah's boss, but I was only a few years older than her, so it wasn't long before started getting lunch together and hanging out outside of the office. We became fast friends and now, almost four years later, she's still one of my closest friends and my go-to person when something exciting, sad, frustrating, or even boring happens in my life. After working with me for a summer, Hannah went back to Clark University (no relation to me, although sometimes I pretend that I own that school and I'm not a millionaire yet because they forgot to pay me my royalties). The entire time I've known Hannah, she has worked a minimum of two jobs to be able to pay her bills and graduate on time. She worked as an RA in her school to cut down cost of living expenses while interning at various companies to build her resume. She even has her own business, The Fashion Cookbook, that started as a blog and grew to the point of being able to hire her own interns.

Last year, Hannah's hard work and friendliness also caught the eye of her professor, Rachael, who knew that although Hannah was working her butt off, she wouldn't be able to live on campus the following year while she finished her graduate program. So, Rachel offered Hannah a place to live rent-free in exchange for babysitting her two young children.   Hannah spent the year babysitting and carpooling, completing her graduate classes and working a full-time internship in Boston at New Balance. Through that internship, she met Joy Clair who connected Hannah with her friends at Adidas in their celebrity showroom/ influencer marketing. About a month ago, as I started writing this book, Hannah bought a one-way ticket to Los Angeles to interview for an internship with Adidas. Oh and, while she's out there, she'll be living with a friend of a friend whom she met through Facebook. Spoiler alert, Hannah got the internship at Adidas *and* got a job doing social media at a creative agency. She is doing what she has wanted to do for years. I'm so happy for her and so proud of her. Hard work really does pay off. I take back what I said earlier about all you need is a connection. All you need is a connection, hard work, dedication, and sometimes, your heart whispering "you can do it, now's the time." Make connections, take risks and see where it will take you.

Lessons Learned

We are not our parents. Although there are some similarities (we are people after all) but comparing millennial issues to baby boomer issues is like comparing apples to oranges – and that's ok. We may not have the security that our parents had after graduating high school or college, but we have the advantage of being able to adapt and use the skills we've acquired to work several different jobs/careers if necessary. Don't get caught up in comparing where you are now with where your parents were when they were your age. Live beyond comparison. You'll be a lot less stressed. Also, don't drink wine for dinner – it will not end well.

Adulting Tactic #2

Security. It is a scary word but only when you don't have it. If you have a sense of security, whether it is a roof over your head and food to eat or a cushy job with benefits and good pay, you feel a lot better. Think for a minute: What do you have? If you're ever feeling like that safety net is gone (or never existed for you in the first place), or your anxiety of the future is overwhelming or you're feeling like you're struggling just to survive the now, make a list of what you DO have. What is something that is great in your life? Even if it's the fact that you know where your next meal will come from or that you have a warm bed to sleep in at night, write it down. Write down all the good, take a moment to be grateful for what you do have, and you'll feel that cozy blanket of security appearing over your shoulders. Create the feeling of security, and you'll be less likely to stress over outside factors that you can't control.

Entrepreneurship

"Make your passion your paycheck." Unknown

Imagine a weekday where you can go grocery shopping at 2pm when there is practically no one else at the store. You can take your time finding what you need and checking things off your list, rather than rushing through crowds or not getting an ingredient because there are five people with carts all blocking what you need. Imagine having a pay check that you felt you really earned, and you can be proud of it. Imagine making your own schedule and being able to take days off for events that you may have missed out on in the past. To me, that's entrepreneurship: being your own boss and making your own decisions.

Even though 60-80% of millionaires are self-made, according to entrepreneaur.com, the term "entrepreneur" is still seen as a negative term. Maybe because some people cover the term "unemployed" with "entrepreneur" or "lazy" with "self-employed." Take my career for example. I love my job, I love making my own schedule, and I love the income and leadership opportunities I've had over the years. Yet even though I'm clearly very happy with what I do and have been doing it for over five years, people still are shocked when I say it's my full-time job, or they ask,

"When are you going to get a 'real' job?" I'm pretty sure I get a real pay check every week. Just because I don't commute to an office and stay in a cubicle for 8 hours a day doesn't mean I don't have a real job.

The point is, do whatever makes you happy. If you're not happy pouring coffee or waiting tables, know that it's a temporary solution until you have your dream job, or leave, find a different job, or create a different job. If you are happy with your job, then stay there, keep kicking ass and block out the nay-sayers. Don't listen to the critics who want you to be miserable just because they are and think that all work should be miserable.

Lessons Learned

When it comes to your job - something you spend the majority of most days doing and get paid for – you have to do what makes you happy.

If your dream is to get paid to create art, or build a business from scratch, know that you, and only you, can make that decision and determine if it's a "good" job. There's no insta-entrepreneurship. It will take time; sometimes double or triple the time you were expecting. But, like hiking, even if you're going slowly, you're still moving upward. And, like hiking, the time and energy put into the hike leads to a better view. It won't always be easy, but if it's your dream job, it will be worth it. The long hours, absurd frustrations and possible tears will be worth it in the end if you stick with it.

Adulting Tactic #3

What is your dream job? Maybe you have no idea what your dream job is, but you'd like to figure out what it is. Maybe you know what your dream job will NOT be. For example, after working in a restaurant for a few years, I learned that my dream job does NOT involve being on my feet all shift or running up and down stairs with heavy trays. For some, the thrill of restaurant life is something to aspire to, and I can now appreciate it, but would not want to have to do it every day.

To guide you in figuring out if the entrepreneurial lifestyle is one you'd like, I've made a flow chart for you. In true millennial spirit, you can use crayons to fill out the chart. Or you can be a daring adult and use pen. Follow the flow chart below (or create your own) and write out all your hobbies for which you could get paid.

29

From there, fill in the squares – how you could make that hobby a career? Or how could you find a job that includes that hobby?

Next are the circles – the necessary steps to achieving that. If you want your hobby to stay a hobby, that's fine, but if your dream job aligns with your hobby, there's going to be work that needs to be done. If you know the steps ahead of time of where you want to go, taking the steps at the appropriate times is then easier.

If you're filling out this chart and realize you're already pretty far along in the dream job process, Keep Going! If you can barely think of the first step, maybe put the chart aside, think about it, and go back to it later. This isn't fifth grade where you get in trouble for not filling out the chart the correct way. You don't HAVE to do this, but it could be a helpful tool in your tactics.

1. List Hobbies You Enjoy, for Which You Could Be Paid:

➢ Photography
➢ Dancing
➢ Writing

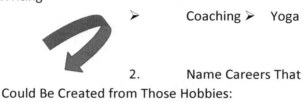

➢ Coaching ➢ Yoga

2. Name Careers That Could Be Created from Those Hobbies:

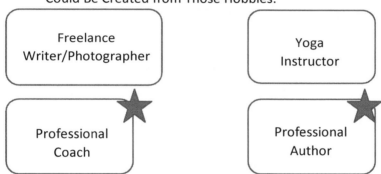

Freelance Writer/Photographer

Yoga Instructor

Professional Coach

Professional Author

3. Star the career you like most, then brainstorm the next steps you need to take to make these careers happen:

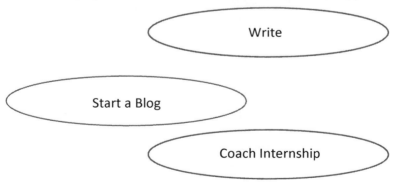

Write

Start a Blog

Coach Internship

1. List Hobbies You Enjoy, for Which You Could Be Paid:

➢

➢

➢

➢

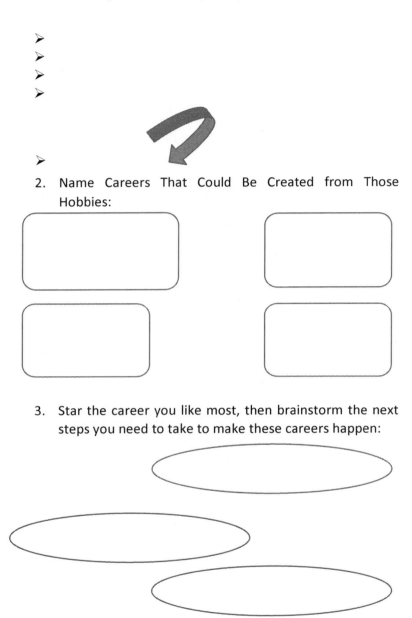

➢

2. Name Careers That Could Be Created from Those Hobbies:

3. Star the career you like most, then brainstorm the next steps you need to take to make these careers happen:

Finances

"Beware of little expenses. A small leak can sink a great ship." ~
Benjamin Franklin

Almost no one in my generation has a clue as to how to be financially responsible. Savings are non-existent, living paycheck to pay-check is the norm and talking about anything past the basics (getting into IRAs, investing etc.) is pointless because twenty-somethings can't focus on long term goals when they're scared they're not going to be able to pay rent. Financial education classes weren't taught in my high school and as an English major in college, I literally had to take one math class for one semester my freshman year (and I passed by the skin on my teeth) so I didn't even have an opportunity to learn how to save or where to invest. I learned from watching my overly frugal Dad and working for an amazing marketing company that taught that kind of stuff. It wasn't until my first conference, when I was 21 years old, is when I learned about compound interest and my brain exploded. I didn't open a credit card until this year and am just now learning how important building good credit is.

One friend recently got married, at 26, and she and her husband have zero savings. How scary is it to plan your life with someone, think of all the things you want to do; travel, have kids etc., but have absolutely no money to do that?

Another time, I was talking to one friend about my saving goals and said that I was disappointed in myself because I wasn't able to contribute what I wanted to my ROTH IRA.

She looked at me as if I had 10 heads. She had never heard those words before, ever.

I'm definitely not an expert on this subject but I do consider myself to be frugal – as I'm writing this, I'm sitting in a Starbucks, drinking my own tea that I brought from home- and I have a savings account with more than $100, so I'm statistically better off than the average American. According to Creditdonkey.com, "The number of Americans who have no cash in the bank to fall back on is staggering. Approximately 26% of adults have no savings set aside for emergencies, while another 36% have yet to start socking away money for retirement" and "Almost half of Americans would not be able to cover an unexpected expense of $500 or less. Almost a quarter would not be able to cover even $100. An estimated 22.9% of men and 22.7% of women say they don't have at least a Benjamin in their emergency fund." And that's an average for adults. The statistics for millennials are even more shocking. "Millennials, on the other hand, meaning adults who are 35 and under, have a personal savings rate of negative 2%. Between high student loan debt and stagnating wages, saving anything at all proves to be impossible for many of them."

Nearly impossible is an understatement.

How many stereotypes about the "broke college student" can you think of? What's troubling though is that the jokes and stereotypes are a scary reality for most. It's almost as if surviving solely off of ramen noodles and Pop-Tarts and growing your hair long because haircuts are too expensive is the new coming of age necessity.

How did we get this way? How did being broke become the norm? Well to start, most of us just don't know any better because we simply weren't taught. As I mentioned, I learned frugality from my father and finances from my company, but I never had to take course on budgeting or investing in high school or college. I still joke about being bad with math, but I honestly think that the last time I was taught necessary math (things that I would actually use in everyday life) was in 5th grade. And it's not that my school was bad, it's just that the focus of education was more on increasing test scores than life lessons. I had great teachers, and I remember some things (the Pythagorean Theorem: A2+B2=C2) but no one ever taught me that you're going to save thousands of dollars a year if you bring your own lunch to work rather than buying a sandwich every day. I think common sense courses, where they teach you how to balance a check book and about credit should be mandatory, but until I become president and the American educational system is drastically changed, you're going to have to live with my advice.

Again, I'm not an expert, but I can tell you that it doesn't have to be this way! It is possible to save and invest money, even at a young age.

This book is supposed to be informative, and because I'm not an expert, I decided to reach out to an expert and get some good advice for you guys.

John Wasserman is a business man, a legend in my business, an author, a husband and father, and most importantly for this section of the book, a financially stable adult. I reached out to him with some specific questions, and he delivered the goods:

1.   If you could tell someone graduating high school your best three tips on how to save money, what would you say?

> *Create an emergency fund of $500-1000. Use only for emergencies. "It's 2am and I need cheese fries" is not an emergency. If you do dip into your emergency fund, create a plan to replenish it right away. Most people miss this step and end up draining their emergency fund, and then they go into credit card debt when the next "emergency" happens.*

> *Don't get a credit card, get a debit card instead. Don't spend money you don't have. Stay out of debt. And if you have debt, work extra hours and pay it off ASAP. It's infinitely easier to build wealth when you have no debt.*

> *Invest 15% of every paycheck. Your 65-year-old self with thank you. Start this as early in life as possible.*

2.   What was the smartest financial decision you made when you were young that led you to your financial freedom now?

I married someone that was financially responsible. (What I believe he is saying here, is not that you have to marry someone financially savvy, but that it will certainly help in you having more success with your finances if you and your significant other are on the same financial 'page'.)

3.   How important is credit/ what's the best way to build credit?

Don't fall into the credit score trap. You don't need a credit score. You can find a broker to underwrite a mortgage for your home purchase. You simply need to pay your bills on time so you can show a history of responsibility. Now, with that said, if you do want to work on a credit score (which is actually a reflection of your relationship with debt, not necessarily credit), the best thing to do is pay off your card each month. If you do have a balance, keep it under 20% of your credit limit. For example, if you have a card that will allow you to charge $2000, don't let your balance get over $400.

4.   What are your top three books to recommend to young people who wish to learn more about how to be financially savvy?

1. Deciding to Thrive by John Wasserman. The last two chapters are your blueprint for managing money.

2. The Total Money Makeover, by Dave Ramsey.

3. The Index Card: Why Personal Finance Doesn't Have to Be Complicated, by Harold Pollack and Helaine Olen.

Take Mr. Wasserman's advice and read his book if you want to learn more.

Learning how to be financially savvy can be boring at times. I don't think anyone ever looked forward to a math class or sat in anticipation before going over a monthly budget. But as someone who has experienced being totally broke (having to ask my parents to help pay for my rent when I'm supposed to be an independent young adult, was one of the most embarrassing/ humbling experiences of my life) and as someone who has been able to watch a savings account grow, I can tell you that it's definitely worth it, and money is definitely important. And, I can also tell you that *it gets better.* Really, it does.

How does it get better? You ask, do I really get to buy fresh fruit and vegetables instead of living off pop-tarts and ramen noodles? Is there actually light at the end of this tunnel? Yes.
If you make the right decisions.

First of all, your perspective of money changes as you grow older. Remember when you were a kid and $1 in a birthday card seemed like a lot of money? Now, most of us would agree that $1 isn't going to buy us much. You can't even buy a bottle of water with a one-dollar bill anymore. What do you think is a lot of money? If someone gave you $50 would that be a lot of money to you? What about $1000. Whatever you think to be a lot of money now, will seem like chump change in 10 years. Once you experience paying bills or buying college text books or buying a car, your concept of money, how you budget/save or spend grows and evolves. Let me share with you the mattress story: I love my sleep. Where most people can function on 4-6 hours of sleep, I need a minimum of eight to be a functioning human. I have a wonderful superpower which is the ability to fall into a dead sleep for any amount of time. If my alarm clock doesn't go off, or if I'm just kind of sleep deprived from work or something, I'll turn off my alarm and I will not wake up

to eat healthy and buy local organic food when I can. I also know that if I spend a little more on good food now, I will spend less in the long run when it comes to healthcare.

➢ Insurance. Having been in car accidents and finding out that my insurance will pay for a rental car so I can get to work while my car is being fixed, or finding out that I don't have to worry about paying for something else because my insurance company will take care of it is the adult equivalent as someone giving you a big hug and saying: *It will all be ok.* If you own anything of value, your piece of mind is worth a few dollars more a month.

Things that I very rarely spend money on/try to not spend money on:

➢ Toilet paper. I have a confession. I haven't spent more than $10 on toilet paper in 3 years! When I go to do laundry at my parent's house, I take a few rolls, I know, I'm very sneaky. I'm aware that it's kind of weird for me to be a toilet paper thief, and I know that toilet paper really isn't that expensive, but if I don't have to spend money on something, I won't. If I have to go to the store and buy toilet paper, I buy the store brand because spending more than $4 on something you're literally going to flush down the toilet is baffling to me.

➢ Eating out. Unless it's a special occasion, or a monthly treat, I try not to spend money on restaurants. There was a time when I was driving around, going from sales call to sales call, stopping for a coffee in the morning, a sandwich or salad at a delicious bread restaurant and then getting take out for dinner. No wonder why I was complaining about being broke. I was literally eating all of my money. Not only do I save money by cooking meals at home or brewing my own coffee, I enjoy restaurants more because it's more like a treat to myself rather than a daily expense.

➢ Materialistic expenses. I've been using the same purse for 5 years. It holds my stuff, which is what purses are for. I simply don't care about being a fashionista. I know some people really care about fashion and owning a Louis Vuitton hand bag is a status symbol in addition to being a fashion statement, but I'd rather spend $500 on a flight somewhere than a purse. If fashion was a hobby of mine, I can see the value in it, but it's just not something that is a priority for me.

➢ Name brand pharmacy purchases. Body wash, shampoo, toothpaste, even make up. The body wash that I buy at the dollar store instead of the $10 brand name cleans just as well. Even basic medicine. Look at the ingredients and dosage. The store-brand ibuprofen is the exact same thing as Advil. Wal-dryl is the exact same thing as Benadryl. Men's black razors work just as well, if not better, than the pink razors that are sometimes double in price. Don't be fooled by name brands and fancy colors. Putting a pink label on something and directing it towards women so it can have a higher price tag on it is the oldest marketing trick in the book.

➢ Anything that I don't NEED. Learn the difference between needing something and wanting something. There are very few things that we as humans need. Sometimes we want something that will make our lives easier and we convince ourselves that we actually do need it.   But just as John Wasserman said, "its 2 am and I need cheese fries is not an emergency", you don't NEED those fall boots just because every other girl on your campus has cute fall boots.   Learn to prioritize, your bank account and future self will thank you.

Food

"One cannot think, love, sleep well if one has not dined well."
Virginia Woolf

Ok, it's time to talk about one of my favorite subjects; food. I love food dearly. My relationship with food has evolved quite a bit over the years. I've been the teenager avoiding meals in fear of gaining two pounds and the twenty something gluttonous and avoiding the gym because ice cream and movies seemed better. Now I like to think I'm at a healthy middle ground. I still have a sweet tooth and will make brownies just to eat the batter occasionally, and sometimes over indulge on wine (it has antioxidants, ok!) but over-all I eat clean and I take care of my body and what goes into it.

Another stereotype of my generation is that as soon as someone goes to college, they gain the dreaded freshman 15, and unfortunately this is yet another thing that is often true. It's not that there are no healthy options in dining halls, some schools have made great strides in having local, organic, healthy options. The reason students, especially freshmen, gain weight is because they don't know how to manage stress, get enough sleep, drink enough water and especially eat well and all those factors lead to weight gain. And why is this? We. Were. Never. Taught. Unless someone is in the health field or a nutrition major, the most they learn about food and nutrition is vegetables good, burgers bad.

I'm happy to learn that some elementary schools are changing school lunches and teaching young kids about food and where it comes from. But for those of you reading this who are over the age of eight but are still overwhelmed by floods of information out there, but don't know what sources are good and what sources are bad, or if you've tried eating "healthy" but still have trouble reaching your health goals (or are thinking health goals? What?!), I have done a fair amount of research and have many friends who are health nuts and again, I asked a few experts here.

My friend Ian is a successful entrepreneur, D-1 athlete, nationally ranked dancer and all around smart guy. He has been a vegan for many years and is one of my go-to's for nutrition advice. WARNING! Some of his advice is on the extreme side. One of his philosophies in life is why do anything if you're not going to really go for it? So, healthwise, he goes for the gold, as I believe we all should. Again, this section is not all inclusive. You don't have to read this and suddenly change your diet to being completely vegan. In fact, I would highly advise against that. If you read this and think "hmm ok, I can try that vegan thing" gradually take things out of your diet, research plant-based protein, consult your doctor or nutritionist and see if it's right for you. I'm not a vegan, but I do follow most of his advice. For example:

1. The 80-20 rule. Make 80% of what you eat vegan. 20% doesn't matter. If you're at a restaurant and all they have is steak, eat a steak. But it's a myth that you NEED meat in your daily diet.

My version of the rule is 80% of the time, I eat as well as I can, 20% of the time I allow treats. I don't call them "cheat" days because I don't consider it cheating, I consider it eating. But If I'm on vacation or if it's a special occasion, I'll indulge. Don't deny yourself something you love, that will only make resisting it harder.

2. Don't eat anything processed. Avoid plastic wrapping. If you can't pronounce all the ingredients on the label, don't eat it. Processed food is filled with sugar and sugar is basically poison for your body.

3. Track what you eat.
   Sometimes we think we're eating well but once we write down and realize exactly what we're consuming, we realize we're over-eating or not actually eating healthy. If you are looking to lose weight, what you eat is 200% more important than going to the gym.

4. Drink water. Ian chugs a class of water with fresh with lemon every morning. This is a habit I've adopted. It cleans you out, flushes toxins, wakes you up, and hydrates you. And STAY HYDRATED. Keep drinking water throughout the day. Gross but true trick, look at your pee. If it is any kind of yellow, you are dehydrated. So many people are dehydrated and don't realize it. Hydration is so important for weight loss, healthy hair skin and skin, avoiding headaches, and also our ability to focus.

Finally, I asked Ian what he believes to be the biggest misconception about eating healthy. His response: that it's hard. And he's right. People are afraid to eat healthy because it seems like a lot of work. It's not. It just comes down to making one good decision after another.

Lessons Learned

What you eat matters. The food you eat can affect everything; from your weight to your energy levels and over all happiness. You don't have to constantly eat salads, but the more good food your body gets, the better off you'll be. You can indulge occasionally, but like many things, it's about balance. Find the balance that works for you. Eating well doesn't have to be hard. In fact, in my years of being a vegetarian and eating healthy, I've found it's much easier than I was making it out to be when I was stressing out about what I was going to eat. Just make a good decision, then another and if you make a bad decision, use your resources to get back on track.

Adulting Tactic #4

➢ If you've ever neglected to plan out what you're going to eat for the day or week then have chosen a not-so healthy food just because it was fast and convenient, maybe it's time to give planning a try. After you've planned out your week with other obligations (when you're working, studying, etc.), add in the food. Write out your breakfast options for the next few days, then lunch, dinner, and plenty of snacks. I have a separate notebook dedicated to food, but you can put your food plan in with your regular calendar, too.

➢ After you've planned what you're going to eat, track what you've eaten. You can't improve what you don't know. Some people use a food journal for this, there are also many helpful apps out there. I've been using My Fitness Pal for years, and although I don't always agree with the calorie recommendation, I love how it tracks my nutrients and exercise all on my phone.

➢ Find a food accountability buddy. If it's difficult for you to make healthy choices, talk to someone in your peer group who often makes healthy choices. Learn from them and if you go out to lunch, it'll be easier for you to choose the healthy option if someone else does, too.

Erin A. Clark

Time management

"Don't get side-tracked by people who are not on track" Unknown.
This scenario might be familiar to you: At the beginning of
the semester, or week (or any time frame, really), you are
assigned a paper or project or something important. You say
to yourself "Ok, this time, I'm not going to wait until the last
minute. I'm going to be productive." But then life happens.
You get invited to a party with your friends and you say,
"play now, work later." Then you have a busy day of classes,
work, more classes, running errands, and before you know
it, it's 9pm and you're exhausted. Once again, you say "I'll
do it tomorrow." And then life happens again, and again and
the thing you were supposed to be working on this whole
time is suddenly due tomorrow and you have to scramble
to get it done. Maybe you get a double shot of espresso and
pull an all-nighter even though you know you need your
rest. Maybe you have to put off other things because now
this is suddenly a priority. And maybe you do an ok job on
the project because you claim you "work better under
pressure." But you know that you could have done better if
you had taken more time to prepare.

When I was in high school, I was definitely guilty of this. In
college, it happened too. But when I was in college, I was
usually very organized and managed my time exceptionally
well. Mostly because I had so much going on that I had to
write stuff down and follow a schedule. I was a full-time
student, I was a tutor, an orientation leader, I exercised and

49

went to the gym, I had friends and relationships I wanted to maintain, I had started working at my sales job and later took on management opportunities. I had so much to do, that I didn't have time to procrastinate. I made my schedule at the beginning of every week and if it said, "work on Lit. paper," I knew I had to do that at that time because I wouldn't have another chance to do it otherwise, and it wouldn't get done. I had the positive pressure of not wanting to let anyone, especially myself down, so this worked for me. I rarely missed an assignment, I never missed a meeting, and I did well in my classes, excelled in my job and was excited about the flow, the daily grind. I was busy, but I was balanced. I still had time for my friends, I still had occasional days off where I could have a "me" day, and I felt that I was succeeding, so I didn't mind putting the work in.

Then I graduated and worked in management. I had a lot to do, all the time. I lived in the middle of nowhere and I didn't have friends or school or anything in my schedule other than work, so that's all I did. I often worked 12 to 13-hour days. I'd get home to my tiny apartment, go to sleep and get up and start it over again. At first, I loved it. I loved recruiting and teaching reps to be successful in sales like I was. And at first, I loved the amount of work I was putting into it. But then, my excitement dwindled, and with it, my results. I was still working the long days, recruiting and advertising and doing everything for my business, but I wasn't getting the results I wanted. It was downward spiral of not being excited, doing the work, asking myself why I was doing all that work for such little results, convincing myself to be positive, working more, getting worse results, then not having money because of my lack of results, working more....

On and on and on for about a year. Management was a good opportunity for me. I learned a lot about business and a lot about myself. There were many times when I thought to myself "If I can get through this day, I can do anything" and I'm a stronger person because of it. But when it got to the point of losing money, and in a way, wasting time, I decided to close my office and move back home. I didn't see that as a failure because I knew how much I had grown from this experience. It was time to end that chapter of long days and office responsibilities, so I packed everything up and loaded the U-Haul back to New Hampshire.

Then I had nothing in my schedule. At all. For the first time in my life I didn't have to do anything at any particular time. Because I was living back home with my parents, I didn't have to pay rent and because I didn't have an immediate need for money, I worked as little as possible. I convinced myself that because I worked so hard the last year, I deserved a rest. At first, I was only going to rest for a week, "I'm taking this week off, and I'll get back to doing appointments and working after I recharge." That week turned into about two months of literally nothing. I'd wake up around noon, watch Netflix for a few hours, eat something bad for me, watch more TV or movies and then go to bed. As I'm writing this, I'm trying to remember if anything significant happened at all in that time period, and I can't remember anything. That time is just a void in my memory because I simply wasted it.

Now, I'm at a healthy balance again. I think in life we go through phases of stress. I'm sure that when I have a child someday, I will stress over things that are not even a thought in my brain as a 25-year-old, stress-free entrepreneur, but for now, I'm going to ride this wave.

Maybe down the road, if I am stressed out, or reaching my breaking point, I can look fondly back to this time in my life and remember serenity and I can channel that energy. I make my own schedule and fill it with important things. Things that keep me happy, productive and healthy. I'm succeeding in my business and working less hours. I have more free time to enjoy the days. I schedule happiness first. And if I can't fit it into my schedule, I find small things that make me happy. For example, I'll schedule a day off to do a work out, read, relax, and hang out with friends. If it's a particularly busy week and I know I'm going to have to work a lot, I'll schedule a half a day where I can take a few hours to write. If I can't do that, I'll take 10 minutes in between appointments and client meetings to treat myself to an iced coffee, and just sit and enjoy it. You can find happiness anywhere, you just have to look harder to find it sometimes.

What makes you happy? Schedule that. If live music makes you happy, make it a point to get together with friends once a month and go to a concert. You don't have to spend hundreds of dollars on concert tickets either, by the way, there are tons of free festivals, local pubs that have local bands play local music, etc. Just do a little research for your area. I'm happy when I'm on a nature walk, just thinking or clearing my head, so I try to walk on the trails near my house once a week or so. If spending time with your significant other makes you happy, schedule a date night where you can both be totally focused on each other and the activity you're doing together so the breakup mantra of "we grew apart" doesn't creep in. You'll learn that some things you need every day, some you can do once a year and be totally fulfilled. But whatever it is, make time for it.

Lessons Learned

Plan for happiness first. Schedule trips, vacations or even date night with your significant other so that you have something in your schedule to look forward to. Then plan obligations. Then plan for success or time for growth. As you grow, not only do your standards rise, but also your obligations change. If you plan for some of these ahead of time, you won't be overwhelmed or stressed when change comes.

Adulting Tactic #5

Buy a planner. Nowadays we're lucky to have so many ways to be able to get organized – phones, computers, apps and the traditional pen and paper planner. Use these resources! Personally, I use my phone for important reminders, an oldfashioned notebook planner and notepads where I write my to do lists for each day. When I was in college and had so many obligations, I would write different things in different colors, so I knew exactly what I was working on and when. I once tried a huge wall calendar, so I could see what needed to be done months down the road. If you're a big-picture person, this might be your best system. Find a system that works for you, then most importantly, implement it.

Productivity & Prioritizing

"Nobody is too busy, it's just a matter of priorities." Unknown

Prioritizing is the key to productivity. Prioritize happiness; don't schedule a dentist appointment on a day you have a yoga class that you love to go to if it means you're going to miss that class. That could mean that you miss the yoga class and miss your weekly exercise spot, or weekly "me" time and the rest of the week feels stressful and unhappy. If that's the only time the dentist can fit you in, is there another class you could go to instead? Doing something that makes you happy should be top priority.

Step one to being happy: create happiness; make time for it. That's also step one in creating a productive schedule. When I'm planning my schedule for work, planning out my goals etc., I first write down if I have any trips planned, then I'll plan date nights or friend dates (these don't have to be planned out to the last detail, but I'll confirm with whoever I'm planning that that day works for both of us and I'll block it off in my schedule). Then I'll plan obligations – things I can't miss; a meeting with my manager, an event that I'm working that week, a training seminar one afternoon, writing time etc. For you, these might be classes, study groups, sports practice etc. Don't freak out if your obligations also align with your happy time. You might love your Anthropology class that you have to go to every

Wednesday, that's a good thing! In fact, you should look for the over-lays. For example; I love writing, so I always looked forward to English classes in high school. In college, I still looked forward to these obligatory classes and that's how I decided I wanted my major to be English. And look at me now! Writing a book! (Cue the sappy growing up music. Aww).

Some obligations you are not going to want to, but you know you have to. Do not miss obligations just because you don't like them. I promise, you will learn something. At the very least, you will learn that you don't like something and have no interest in it. Example: I hate math but as an undergrad, I had an obligation to take one basic math course my freshman year. I hated that class, I hated going, but I went anyway because I didn't want to fail. I couldn't tell you any equations or theories from that class today if you paid me a million dollars, but I can tell you that I learned that I'm definitely glad I didn't choose a career where I'd need to use those equations every day. A better example: My sister is going to school to be a pharmacist. As part of her program, she has to take a lot of really intense and fast paced anatomy classes. She doesn't particularly like the homework that comes from those classes (the obligation she has to plan for in her schedule) but she'll learn what body parts are effected by which drugs – kind of important if you're going to be helping patients with their medications as a career. For those of you in sales; you may not like the obligation of making phone calls or contacting clients initially (your obligatory first step), but you know that if you don't make the phone calls, you don't schedule appointments, you don't get a chance to make your phone calls. See what I'm saying?

Good. After I schedule obligations, then I schedule success time. Success time when I was in college was "finishing that project" or "going to the gym" things that, when I complete them, I can feel like I've accomplished something. Some days I like to ask myself, "How can I make today a day where I sit down at the end of it and say to myself: Wow! Today was really productive!" Productive days, to me, are days where I check off every category on my list. Work: accomplished a lot, check. Relationship: had a good time, had some good conversations, check. Health: I had a really good work out and ate well today, check. Happiness: Made time to read, check. These vary day to day, but the goal is to have a check in every box. I do this because I like to feel productive; doesn't everyone?

We don't always like the work it took or the progress, but we like producing good results; athletes can say "I had a productive workout" meaning they accomplished a lot and they're happy with their skills gained (why #gainz is so popular – people like to share great results) or muscle (visible results of hard work).

Sometimes we need to raise our standards of what we consider productive. Five years ago, I considered finishing all of my homework to be productive. And it was, for me, at that time. Now I'm productive when I accomplish more things in one day. As you grow, your standards rise. Example: someone who never goes to the gym or isn't used to working out, might think that walking into the gym building and using the treadmill for ten minutes, as opposed to the professional body builder who is passionate about exercise and could think three hours of continual weight lifting was an average day. I know people who spend hours at the gym, or hours dancing, or hours cooking all in an effort to perfect their craft. And I know people who don't agree with their standards, or simply don't have that interest in common, and say "Well, they're crazy for spending so much time on that."

They're not crazy. They have a crazy, ridiculous work ethic. They achieve crazy results. They have the body everyone dreams of, or they have a beautiful technique named after them, or maybe they can cook the best tasting meal you've ever tried.

Find what you love and work your butt off to have the best version of that. If you love to write, picture yourself as the next J.K. Rowling, arguably one of the most successful authors in recent history. If you love to play basketball, picture yourself as the next Michael Jordan. If you love science, picture yourself as the next Stephen Hawking. After you picture this, do what's necessary to get there.

Prioritizing

Whenever you feel overwhelmed, that comes from feeling like you're losing control or have no control. When you're managing a schedule that includes school, activities, work, more work, homework, time with friends and more your schedule can certainly become overwhelming. Here's what I like to do when I'm feeling like I have so much to do and so little time: Write out everything you have to do. Scribble activities in whichever order they come out. Essay, math homework, laundry, dance class, movies with sister, make lunch, work out...EVERYTHING. Once that's done and you've written down every activity you can think of, go back to your goals. If you've made a goal sheet or even have thought of something you want to have in the near or far future, you have a dream and have some idea of what you want in life.

Put those lists side by side -either physically or picture them in your head — and notice which activities, obligations, haveto-dos, whatevers, line up with those goals. In other words, ask yourself "which of these things that I have to do will get me to my goal, or is a necessary step in getting me to my goal?" Then go through the list of things that are overwhelming you and write a number next to each thing in order of importance. Then, and here's the fun part, follow the three Ds: Delegate, Defer, and Delete. Anything on that list that isn't the number one or number two things (maximum) ask; can I delete this, can I delegate this, or can I defer this?

Delegate anything that is important but could be completed by someone else. Delete anything that is unnecessary and defer anything that if you don't to today and do it tomorrow instead, the world will not explode. For example, if your goal is to nail a job interview or be an overall professional person, clean laundry is important. Appearance and stench matters in the professional and social world, and you most likely will not get hired or taken seriously if you show up wearing ripped, or stained jeans or a shirt that smells like you've worked out in it for a week in a row. But is laundry THE most important thing you have to do right now to get to your goal? If it's an emergency, like you have absolutely no clean underwear left and don't want to risk a not-so-fun infection kind of emergency, then yeah, do your laundry. But if you're good for a few days and you don't absolutely need to do your laundry in order to achieve your goal of getting a 4.0 this semester, then maybe you could defer this activity to tomorrow. Or if buying almond milk is on the list of things that you have to do at some point in the near

Erin A. Clark

future in order to accomplish your goal of eating healthy and starting off the day with a smoothie, but if it's a number five on the list, it still has to get done, but it's not number one or two, maybe you could ask your roommate to pick some up for you when she goes to the store later on. Delegating is not mooching, it's resourcing. You'll pay her back or get her something next time you go to the store. Then delete any unnecessary tasks. Writing things down helps you to realize your priorities. Maybe you were stressed out because it felt like you had SO Much to do.

This helps me when I have a lot to do and when I feel I have nothing to do. It allows me to avoid feeling bored. If I happen to have a day where I don't work or don't have obligations, I can go back to that list and see what I've been deferring. For example, if I've been putting off sending an email for a few days and suddenly I have time in my schedule, I'll use that time to send that email or follow up. Or if I'm waiting in line, I'll use that time to read that article I meant to read but couldn't because more important things came up. I never feel like I'm wasting time. Productive time is not time wasted.

Lessons Learned

You are in control of your emotions. If you're feeling overwhelmed or like there just isn't enough time to get everything you need to do done, take a breath, remember that you have the same hours in the day as Beyoncé, and know that stressing out about having too much to do is a good problem to have.

I now try to plan ahead as much as possible because I've found that when I'm prepared, I'm less stressed. My own

59

personal lesson learned is to look ahead instead of focusing on the one thing that's stressing me out. I'll sometimes ask myself "is what I'm stressing out about going to matter in 5 years?" If the answer is no, I stop stressing. If the answer is yes, I do everything that I can to plan/ prepare then I stop stressing.

Adulting Tactic #6

If remembering that you are awesome and in-control of your emotions isn't quite working for you, and you're still feeling overwhelmed, try to write it out way. Write down everything that needs to be done, number those items from most important to least important, then practice the three Ds: Delete, Delegate and Defer

Undeniable Truths

"Every experience is seen through your mind's eye, so when you change your mind, you change your entire world." Bryant McGill

You have to work hard to get what you want. As I previously mentioned, sometimes you have to do things you don't want to do in order to achieve that big picture goal. You don't want to put in the phone calls to meet with clients, but you know that you're not going to meet with any clients or sell any product if you don't make the calls. You don't want to go to the gym, but you're not going to achieve your goal weight, goal body if you sit on the couch.

Many of us know what we have to do to be successful. But why are there so many people not succeeding? It's because we fear. We don't fear success, of course. We fear failing. We fear we won't be successful. We fear we're going to let someone down, especially ourselves. We fear wasting time or wasting money. We fear embarrassment. If you ever shared your dream with someone and they laughed at you or doubted you, for any reason, you may have felt ashamed or embarrassed. As humans, we don't like that feeling, so most shrink away from it and avoid it. The little girl who shared with her classmates that she wanted to be a famous dancer and got laughed at, will be less likely to share those dreams again and if she keeps avoiding that, will be less likely to achieve that goal and she might even forget about it. Another little girl who gets laughed at might get mad and use that as a motivation to prove those meanies wrong. So why do some people shrink away from fear and some use that as a motivator or as inspiration? Those who shrink were never given the tools necessary to overcome adversity.

Many times, people get stuck in a routine of bad habits, or stuck in a job they don't like, or even stuck in a relationship with the wrong person. It's because we get comfortable and we fear stepping out of our comfort zones. But it's when we're challenged to step out of that cozy comfort zone that we are forced to act on what we want. Graduating college and opening my own business was one of the scariest things I've ever done. Had I not had mentors encouraging me, I probably would have stayed in my hometown, and would have waited to venture out into the real world. But I was encouraged to try something new. And as I mentioned, I didn't succeed in the way that I wanted to. But I learned so much about business, about myself, about what I'm capable of.

Think of many popular movies, too. When the protagonist is challenged or forced out of their comfort zone, forced in to change is when they embrace it and their story is developed further. Reese Witherspoon's character in "Wild" lost her mother, was recently divorced and basically struggling to stay afloat. So she went on this amazing journey to hike the Pacific Crest Trail. Julia Robert's character in "Eat, Pray, Love" also found herself at a crossroads and went on a journey of self-fulfillment.

Now, you don't necessarily have to go on a six month hike and throw your boot off the mountain or travel to Bali and Italy just to find yourself, although you'll definitely learn a lot from those experiences. But you should still step out of your comfort zone. Teach yourself to embrace the unknown or uncomfortable now, so that when you're really challenged and have no choice but to embrace it, you'll be able to face adversity head on.

In my business, we have what are known as "push periods." The name is misleading, we're not pushing each other around or being pushy with clients, but we're pushing ourselves and seeing what we're capable of. There's usually some sort of contest associated with these. Sell $6,000 in 10 days and win a trip, sell $10,000 in two weeks and win a limo night in Boston and a Vitamix blender, the prizes vary. If you're reading this and thinking, "Well, Erin. You're drinking the Kool-Aid. They're obviously just trying to motivate you to sell more of the product," you're not wrong. Yes, it is to motivate sales representatives to sell more. And yes, in those two weeks we sell A LOT. But that's not the only reason these contests exist. I've been with this company for over five years and have participated in many push periods. Sometimes I exceed my goal, sometimes I hit it, but just barely (one time the contest was to sell $6000 in

10 days to win a trip to the Bahamas. I sold $6,200, so I just went over, and I won the trip!) And sometimes, I fell short. The times where I fell short by $300 or had everything that could have possibly gone wrong in a week go wrong and still surpassed my goal was when I learned the most. I learned to embrace adversity. I learned more skills from attending more meetings and seminars and simply being more committed. What's most important for the purpose of this book? That I learned how to set goals.

Undeniable Truth #1: Goal Setting is Imperative.

What do you want and why do you want it?

The first step to achieving your goals is setting them and being clear on what you want and why you want it. You can't achieve something you can't see. Take some time to visualize what achieving this goal would mean for you. In his book "Slow Burn", Stu Mittleton discusses the power of visualization. Mittleton is a successful marathoner who coaches others to do so, too. He says "With the vision of the future firmly embedded in your imagination, your mind will lead your body to the fulfillment of your thoughts." I've used vision boards in the past. It's fun to day dream about what's possible. Think about your why. Why are you going after what you're going after? Why are you going to do all the work that's necessary to achieve that goal? For me, a sales contest means I'll sell a lot and as a sales person who is paid by commission, that means I'll make more money. When I first started working in sales, I was embarrassed to say that money was a motivator. Some people are purely motivated by money, and that's not necessarily a bad thing. It could be a bad thing if you're greedy. But using money as a motivator to achieve something bigger is not greedy. For me, I'm not motivated only by money, but I can tell you from experience that I'm a lot more motivated when I have money. For example, if I sell $10,000 in two weeks, and I make 50% commission, I know that I will earn $5,000. What can I do with that? I could max out my Roth IRA for the year, I could put it towards a trip and achieve another goal of traveling to another country. I could donate to a charity. I could buy amazing gifts for my family and friends for Christmas. Imagine what's possible. Maybe your goal is to raise $3000 from a bake sale. What does that mean for you? What do you gain? You'll probably gain organizational and sales skills necessary to achieve that goal. You'll learn to overcome challenges. Maybe you'll be a better role model for a younger brother or sister. Once you establish what you want and WHY you want it, write it down.

By the way, your goals should scare you a little. If you set a goal, but know you can easily achieve it, why go after it? Challenge yourself, step out of your comfort zone. If you've ever made a goal for yourself and said, "could I really do that?" you're on the right track. If you then say, "I don't know if I can, but I am sure gonna try" then you're not only on the right track, but you're up and running.

Write it down and share it as much as possible.

You're 85% times more likely to achieve a goal if you write it down. There's something about putting a goal on paper that is significant beyond measure. When I'm going after a big goal, I'll write it down on sticky notes and stick those anywhere I'm going to see them; on my fridge, on my car steering wheel, on my bathroom mirror. I want it in my face so I can't run away from it.

It's also important to share your goals. Share your goals with anyone who will listen. Know that some people will laugh at you and might not take you seriously, but some, the ones who matter most, will support you no matter how crazy your goals are. When I'm in a sales contest, I even share my goals with my customers. I say "Hey, can I take a minute to share with you why I'm doing this?" The customer usually says yes. It takes less than a minute, but it lets them know that I'm not just trying to sell them something. I'm not a nameless, pushy sales person, I have dreams and aspirations and they can help me achieve them or help me donate to a charity I'm working for.

Make it measurable.

Instead of "I want to lose weight," ask yourself how much weight you want to lose. How many inches of fat do you want to lose? How much muscle do you want to gain? What do you want to look like? Break your goal down to the ridiculous. Going back to my sales contest example, if I want to sell $10,000 in two weeks, how much do I have to sell each week? How much do I have to average per day? How many appointments is that going to take to get there? How many phone calls am I going to have to make to schedule those appointments? How many emails and am I going to have to send out marketing to my customers? I break it down to the ridiculous and plan it out so that I know exactly what I have to do and then when it comes time to execute, I don't have to think, I just follow the plan.

Give it a deadline.

Goals are dreams with deadlines. It's great to say "I want to lose weight" or "I want to buy a new car" or "I want to sell _____ amount" but when do you want to achieve that by? With push periods, it's easy because the contest dates are set. But I've learned to give my goals deadlines – I want to be in the company's hall of fame by 2020, for example.

Learn to give your dream a deadline. If you say "I want to own a house someday" or "that's something I'd like to do someday" someday will most likely never come.

If you're scared about going after something, ask yourself:
"What is the worst that can happen?"

"What's the worst that can happen?" If you fall short of your goal, what are the consequences? Sometimes those consequences are severe and can motivate you even more. For example, if your goal is to pass all of your classes by the end of the semester and the consequence of not achieving that goal is that you lose your scholarship or be on academic probation, you will probably be more likely to work hard to achieve that goal. But sometimes the consequences aren't that bad. Fortunately for me, if I don't hit my sales goal, I don't lose my job or get fired, so I don't have that hanging over my head. So if my goal is $10,000 and I work really hard and only sell $8,000, I don't lose anything. Sometimes having nothing to lose is more motivating. If you don't have anything to lose, why not go for it? If your goal is to lose 30 pounds and you start going to the gym regularly, develop healthy eating habits and work hard, and only lose 10 pounds, you still lost weight, you still worked hard, you still developed those good habits, and you didn't waste anything.

Dream big, go after that big scary goal. But be clear on what you want, write it down, share it often, make it measurable, give it a deadline and go for it, acknowledging the consequences of achieving it and not achieving it.

Undeniable Truth #2: People will always surprise you.

People will always surprise you. Always. This could be bad; For example, that boy that you thought was really nice and seemed really interested in you turned out to be a bit of a player. He surprised you and may have hurt you, but you learn from that. But sometimes when people surprise you, that can be a good thing. When I was a manager, I hired a former felon. In the interview, he was open with me and told me what happened was in the past and he was hoping to grow from that and turn his life around. He also told me how difficult it was to get a job because people saw that on an application (by state law he was required to answer yes if he had ever been convicted of a crime) and wouldn't hire him. There was no policy, that I was aware of, that said I couldn't hire him, so I gave him a chance. Despite his criminal background and the fact that he wasn't a typical college student (most people who I recruited were college students), he came to training, completed his assignments early and outsold everyone in his training group. Now he is happily married and has a beautiful daughter. Similarly, I've gone on sales calls to the nicest house in the neighborhood, with a fancy car parked in the driveway, pool and tennis court in the back yard, you name it. Thinking that I'd definitely leave with a big sale, I assumed the owner would buy a lot. But that's not always the case. One customer lived in such a house, but was going through a sad and horrible divorce with her husband. Needless to say, purchasing knives and cookware was the furthest thing from her mind. You can't judge someone based off of their past mistakes or how they look or where they come from. Everyone has their own story. The expression of "you can't judge a book by its cover" is the most accurate - especially when it comes to meeting new people.

Undeniable Truth #3 – Everything happens for a reason.

One night, when I was 23, I sat outside with my friend. It was a brisk September night, we were sitting on a cold rock, drinking wine and looking up, awaiting the super-moon that we were told was a once in a life time experience.

I remember how incredible the moon looked – like someone had hit zoom on my view of space and made the moon look like a canvas painting. And I remember thinking about how incredible that moment was. We were just sitting outside in a parking lot, but along with the moon, the conversation and the memories that came from that conversation irreplaceable.

At one point, after a few glasses of wine, my friend sighed and said, "Do you think it will ever just make sense?" without hesitation, I said "Yes". I didn't have to ask what she meant by that. I knew without question that the "it" she was referring to was everything - life in general, her situation, her stress, her worry. And then, and now, I know, without question that someday it will all make sense.

There were times where I was so frustrated I wanted to cry but couldn't. And times that I was so stressed out that I wanted to quit, but didn't. There were also many times where I did hide behind my desk and cry. And there were times where I wanted to quit and did. I didn't know it then, but every experience I've ever had, and every experience that I will have, good or bad is a chance to learn.

Everyone experiences stress. Everyone experiences failure, it's how you handle these experiences that matter. You may be in the wrong job or in the wrong relationship or you may be stressed about a class or assignment but if you do what's best for you and take action when needed, it will all work out. If you're asking, "But how do I know what's best?" Ask yourself , "How does it feel?"

If you make a decision and you have a gut feeling that it's a bad decision, then that's not the right decision. Now, the right decision doesn't always feel like rainbows and roses, but it feels right. And unless you're a very intuitive person, it's hard to get a good grip on your gut feeling and listen to what it's telling you. But the good news is, the more correct decisions you make, the easier it is to make right decisions because you acknowledge and recognize when you're making a good decision and you get a better. You make a good decision, then another good decision, then another, then maybe you make a bad decision, but you see it as a learning experience and grow from it, then you make another good decision.

This pattern repeats over and over until one day you look at a picture of who you were when you were experiencing the struggle or the challenge and you think to yourself "Wow, I was a totally different person back then" and you laugh about how stressed you were because everything did eventually work out. Suddenly, it makes sense why you had to go through that. Because you needed that experience to grow from the stressed out, overwhelmed, sad person you were to the energized, productive, happy, influential person you became. And it just makes sense.

Undeniable Truth #4: As you grow, your fears change.

When I was a kid, I was desperately afraid of downstairs darkness. Downstairs darkness is the phenomenon that occurs when you're the last one in a room after others have gone upstairs and you're the last to turn off the lights. I distinctly remember being a kid at my parents' house and calling dibs on using the upstairs bathroom so I wouldn't have to turn off the lights. The reason I was scared then was because I was terrified that whoever or whatever was watching me through the windows (as there surely must have been someone there because that's what my 12-yearold brain told me) would grab me when all the lights were off. I was also scared that if any part of my foot was outside the blanket, whatever was creeping under my bed would grab my ankles and pull me under the bed. Thank you, "Goosebumps" books. I'd run up the stairs and tuck the blanket tight over my feet. Now that I'm an adult, I know that those are illogical fears and can walk up in the darkness or tuck myself in at a reasonable pace (unless of course I'm going up the stairs of a basement, in that case get out of my way!).

When I was 18, then again when I was 22, then again when I was 24, I was so scared of change. And I was scared for the transition because I didn't want to fail. I would joke about putting off high school graduation because I didn't want' to fail in college. I'd joke about the same thing with college graduation because I didn't want to fail in the "real" world. And when it came time to move to a different place and be on my own fully for the first time, I joked that I would be the girl living with her parents even after she was married and had kids of her own because I was terrified of failing as a manager. I didn't like failing and had never really failed in my life before so this unknown scared me. I listened to messages and shared quotes like "conquer your fear" and "embrace the unknown" and then I did that. I conquered my fear, I embraced this unknown new role. And…. I failed. In many ways I learned a lesson and I grew as a person but in a lot of other ways, I fell on my face….in the mud….in front of everyone. But it wasn't that bad. I didn't die. I didn't lose any friends or support. I lost money and I didn't hit my goals, but at the end of the day, I still had a lot to be thankful for and I could pick myself up, dust myself off and move on.

Fear of failure is a very adult fear. Some consider losing money, or not having money to be failure. Many don't go after their dreams because the question of "what if I lose money?" pops up.

My first experience with failure wasn't that bad. By some standards, it really wasn't a failure at all. So now that I'm 25, I can echo the cheesy quotes and Facebook posts and confidently say to my friends and anyone willing to listen "conquer your fears" and "embrace the unknown." But a new fear has grabbed my ankles and left me frightened; the fear of success. Instead of asking "what if I fail?" I've caught myself thinking "what if I succeed but I can't handle it?" or worse "What if I achieve this and it's not what I thought it was?" And I'm working on these fears. I'm talking to people who are successful in their work and seeing that yes, they're successful but that doesn't necessarily mean working 12hour days every day. I'm picturing myself as who I want to be rather than who I fear I'll become.

I'm sure I'll have different fears as things grow and change in my life. Some might be irrational or trivial and some might be genuine and legitimate. But I can't, and you shouldn't, let fear stop you from doing what you want to do.

You simply can't let fear control you. You either learn to live with it or you learn to grow past it. My roommate and dear friend, Megan is the perfect example of this. Megan is not the fearless leader of the group who explores spontaneously. She is the planner. She is the care-giver and sometimes nanny of the group because she is always well prepared with lists, hydration and snacks. I'm forever grateful for her preparedness as she saved my ass on several occasions. When we studied abroad in England, she always had extra granola bars in her purse and made sure all of us had everything we needed (like our IDs, wallets and cellphones) that sometimes got left behind. I first learned Megan had a fear of heights when we all went on the London eye. Megan was almost paralyzed with fear and sat on the bench throughout the ride. But she mustered up the courage to stand near the glass for a quick minute to take a picture because she knew she'd regret letting fear hold her back from that experience.

When I moved in with Megan, I learned that she has a lot of fears other than heights. Some are reasonable and relatable – fear of change, fear of confrontation for example. Some are seemingly illogical and kind of funny – farm animals, being outside at night, camping/wooded areas at any time, loud noises, when I walk into a room without her seeing, the doorbell.

If Megan constantly lived in fear, she would not leave her room. She has adopted many ways to overcome fear or simply live with it. One way to overcome something you're scared of is to just do it. Like the London Eye experience, there was another time when she had to conquer a fear. She had started talking to an old friend from high school and the texting back and forth had turned into an invitation to visit him in New York City. He even bought her a flight to go visit him, such a gentleman! Scared of flying, heights, and change simultaneously, Megan was nervous for the trip, but she was excited and was looking forward to a romantic getaway, that she definitely deserved.

She had planned and re-planned, packed and re-packed, then it came time for her to physically get on the plane. It was then that I got a phone call from Megan. She was speaking quietly and was petrified, and I did the best I could to convince her to go on the plane. I joke with her and her boyfriend now that they can thank me for Megan getting on the plane, but I think that Megan would have done it without my help. Haven spoken to her many times since that happened, I know that she knew deep down that was something she needed to do. "I knew I would regret not taking the opportunity to get something that I had wanted and pictured having for the last ten years."

Since getting on the plane, she and Christopher, started dating and now have a wonderful relationship that single people dream of. Ironically, the relationship has been a long-distance relationship. Which means that both Megan and Christopher fly from city to city every month or so to see each other and Megan flies more often than she ever thought she would. And now, they're preparing to live together and start their lives together. What would have happened if she was really too scared to get on the plane?

As this is something I've really enjoyed thinking and talking about, before starting this chapter, I went to the most legitimate sources for millennials; Facebook. I asked my friends what they're scared of: here are some of the best responses:

"I was afraid of automatic toilets. I overcame it by wearing diapers until 5. Now I fear nothing."

"Bigfoot. Grew out of it? Well, let's just say I don't go on hikes alone."

"I was afraid of the dark until I realized that scary things can happen in the light too. Now I have anxiety about really high, sharp turning freeway ramps."

"When I was young, I feared change, but soon realized that life is endlessly changing and became comfortable with the idea of flowing with the ebb and flow of the tides. I have always feared failure and still do."

"When I was a child I was sometimes afraid something horrible would happen to my parents. When I became a mother, I was afraid something horrible would happen to my children. Not constantly, but with regularity. To overcome this fear, irrational or otherwise, I have put more faith in God. This has helped tremendously! This and the Hal Elrod 'Can't change it!' rule ☺ "

"I'm afraid of fish. I think they look weird and every time they get close I'm scared they're going to attack me like I've seen in the shows. I've done nothing. I'm still afraid of fish.

Lessons Learned

1. You have to work for what you want. Work through fears, work through doubt, work around nay-sayers who try to convince you your goal isn't achievable.
2. Step out of your comfort zone. Teach yourself to embrace challenges now, so that when you have no choice but to face a challenge head on, you will succeed.
3. Set goals clearly. Know what you want AND why you want it. Write your goal down and share it as much as possible. Make your goals measurable - break them down to the ridiculous. Give your goal a deadline.
4. People will always surprise you.
5. Be kind; don't judge. Everyone has their own story.
6. Everything happens for a reason.
7. As time goes on, you grow, your fears change, and you learn to adapt to different situations.

Adulting Tactic #7

Instead of a chart or list to maximize this section, I thought I'd try something different for you. Practice Affirmations. You can go section by section with the Undeniable Truths, or create one positive affirmation that encapsulates all of the categories.

When I encounter an experience that is difficult, or am falling short of a goal, or getting caught up in the comparison game, I write affirmations. You can use these for so many situations. I like to type these out on my phone in the notes section and add to it every so often.

Here are some affirmations that I read aloud/say to myself often. Feel free to use them for yourself or create your own:

- ➢ I am capable of accomplishing anything I desire.
- ➢ Everything happens for a reason. If I don't know the reason, I trust it will work out eventually.
- ➢ I have already gone through so much. This (problem that I'm currently encountering) is nothing compared to that. I am strong.
- ➢ I am deserving of _____ (love, a good job, this prize, hitting my goal).
- ➢ I am kind and non-judgmental.

Add as much as you want and have fun with this list! Refer back to it whenever necessary for a boost of positivity.

Create the Best You

"What you think, you become. What you feel, you attract. What you imagine, you create." Buddha

So now you know what adulting is and how to overcome many challenges that come along with being an adult. You have tips on how to stay focused on your goals and not compare yourself to your peers or older generations. You know how to be financially savvy and how to eat well and take care of yourself. You know about my undeniable truths and have probably created your own as you've grown. You know that your fears change as you grow and how to overcome some of the fears you may have. Now what to do with all that knowledge? Use it to create the best you. Take what you've learned and apply it towards being the best version of yourself.

Take a moment to envision yourself. Not now and how you see yourself, but the future you. And not the future you that is expected by others, because others don't know you and they don't know what happiness is for you. This is 2.0 you. What is she doing? How does she live her life? How does she respond to people? How do other people feel when they're around her? How are you living 10, 15 years from now? Are you a mother or father, a husband or a wife? Are you a home owner? How many homes? What do you do for fun? Do you go on adventures and extraordinary vacations?

Picture it all. Down to the details. If you've always wanted a dog, what is the name of your future dog? Visualization has been studied and practiced by thousands. Good sports players visualize the winning shot. The best sports players visualize the winning shot so many times that they know every detail; down to the hush of the crowd, the smell of sweat.

The reason visualization works so well is because your brain can't tell the difference. Literally. The more you repeat a phrase, the more you picture something, the more likely it is going to happen. This is both good and bad. It's bad if you don't realize how powerful your thoughts are and how much your negative thoughts are impacting your life. Tony Robbins says "The questions you ask control what you focus on. What you focus on controls how you feel. And what you feel is your experience of life."

What questions are you asking yourself? What does the little voice in your head say? We all have that voice. And I've fought with that voice, I think to some extent we all have. There's the voice that says, "You're not good enough" there's the voice that says, "You're going to fail", the voice that says, "You're too _____" we fill in that blank with whatever our insecurities are: too short, too fat, too pale, too shy, too obnoxious, and too frizzy-haired. The list goes on. For a long time, my voice was negative. And for a while, I didn't even realize my voice was negative. I didn't realize that saying things, out loud or to myself, like "I could never do _____ (insert incredibly awesome but kind of scary thing here)" was damaging to my future success.

Recognize a negative thought and replace it with something more positive. What are you saying to yourself? And even more powerful, what do you believe about yourself? If you believe that someday you're going to be a millionaire and jet-setting across the globe, then that will happen. If you believe you're going to have a wonderful home with three kids and a dog, then that will happen.

You create your future. Again, this doesn't happen JUST by thinking. It's not a trick. Your thoughts = your future. Yes. But it's not immediate. What's immediate are your actions. Your thoughts + your actions = your future. Going back to an example that I know; sales. If I think "I'm going to be the best sales rep in the region this week," it will happen. But not because I just say it. I have to say it, visualize it, and then make the decision to act like the best sales rep in the region.
Is the best sales rep watching Netflix instead of prospecting? Probably not.

If you dream of getting all A's this semester, you have to make the extra effort of studying now.

If future you IS fit and healthy, running marathons, winning medals, the current you must choose the apple over the donut.

If future you IS a millionaire, you have to learn how to budget and save your money now.

Step up now, so that later on in life, when you're really challenged, you can step up then and be the most successful, positive, healthy, spiritual, fulfilled person of your dreams. Do what others won't now, so that later, you can do what others can't.

What if you weren't scared?

We all have fears. Fear is natural in humans and has served as an evolutionary advantage. When our cave dwelling ancestors felt fear which meant run from whatever was chasing them so they could survive, procreate and pass on their survival skills to the next generation. Fear was beneficial. In today's world where, most likely, you're not being chased by jungle cats or warring clans, we still have fears, but instead of aiding us, they can cripple us. I've mentioned that as we grow, our personal fears change. And generationally, as we advance, our fears change too. One common fear among our generation is fear of what other people think. We fear judgement and negativity from our peers. These are logical fears because we've grown up in a society where the opinions of others matter. And those opinions are even more in our face because of social media. If you post something on Facebook that you're proud of and then see negative comments, it stings even more. But one thing I've learned in the early years of adulthood is that life goes on whether you listen to criticism or not. The only difference is that you're less likely to achieve your goals if you actually listen to the critics.

I like the saying "what would you do if you knew you couldn't fail?" You'd be unstoppable, right? But to expand on that, what would you do if you weren't scared. Or better yet, what would you do if you were scared, but acted anyway? That's bravery.

Everyone has fears. Use your fears to your advantage. Imagine accomplishing something you've been scared of your whole life. Imagine the person who would come out of that.

It's Going to Be OK!

"You. Wherever you are in this journey. It's going to be okay." Kristin Diversi

Trust me on this one. I know you're stressed. You're dealing with problems that seem trivial to others, but to you it seems like the end of the world. You're trying to figure out typical adult things that no one taught you in addition to trying to find yourself and your passions and your future. If you've made it this far, you already have a better grasp on some issues and hopefully you've learned more about being and adult and being your best self in the process. Pat yourself on the back for that one.

Maybe you've made mistakes that seem unfixable. Or maybe you feel so overwhelmed that you don't even know where to begin to solve the problems. It will all be ok. You have to go through the storm sometimes to see the rainbow. As cheesy as it is, it's true. Everything happens for a reason, even if that reason is that you learn something. If you step back from the problem and ask yourself "Is this issue going to matter in 10 years?" The answer is usually no, and that should help you to not worry about it. But if the answer is yes, then what can you do right now, what's one thing, no matter how small, you can do to start solving? Don't sweat the small stuff.

The more negative your self-talk, the less likely you'll be successful in completing whatever you're trying to do.

Instead of saying "I'm never going to figure this out," say "It'll be nice when I figure this out" or "I can't wait to figure this 'adulting' thing out." That will move you to action and you'll be another step ahead of even actual adults who still don't know what they're doing. You. Will. Be. Fine.

Author's Note:

There were times in my life when I was told this, but never believed it. There were other times where I wasn't told this but needed to hear it. Just like many adult things, some things I had to learn on my own. In the final stages of this book, I'm 27 years old. And in the process of editing, I found an old notebook where I had scribbled some of the original ideas for this book, random thoughts and old dreams from my early 20s. Almost everything I worried about as a 22year-old doesn't matter just 5 years later. Almost every goal I wrote down is now accomplished. It wasn't always easy, but I did it. I hope that you can take some of my advice, learn from my mistakes and be the best you.

Dream big because you can! Accomplish the seemingly impossible because you can! You now know things you possibly didn't learn in high school or college, but you also know that the adult version of you is created *by* you, and he/she has endless potential!

Made in the USA
Middletown, DE
02 September 2021